Let's find
out about...

MY BODY

Studio Manager: Sara Greasley
Editor: Belinda Weber
Designer: Trudi Webb
Production Controller: Ed Green
Production Manager: Suzy Kelly

ISBN-13: 978-1-84898-086-0 pbk

Copyright © ticktock Entertainment Ltd 2010
First published in Great Britain in 2010 by ticktock Media Ltd,
The Old Sawmill, 103 Goods Station Road, Tunbridge Wells, Kent, TN1 2DP

Printed in China
9 8 7 6 5 4 3 2 1

Picture credits (t=top; b=bottom; c=centre; l=left; r=right; OFC=outside front cover; OBC=outside back cover):
ANIMATE4.COM/SCIENCE PHOTO LIBRARY: 13b. Dorling Kindersley: 7t. Dr. Don Fawcett/Getty Images: 5t.
iStock: 18r, 16–17. MEDICAL RF.COM/SCIENCE PHOTO LIBRARY: 13c. Shutterstock: OFCbl, OFCbr, OFCtr, 1, 4,
4–5, 5b, 6l, 6–7, 7br, 8, 9 both, 10–11 all, 12–13, 13t, 14, 15, 16, 17, 18l, 19 both, 20–21 all, 22–23 all, OBC.
Hayley Terry: OFCtl and throughout. M. I. WALKER/SCIENCE PHOTO LIBRARY: 12bl.

Every effort has been made to trace copyright holders, and we apologize in advance for any omissions.
We would be pleased to insert the appropriate acknowledgments in any subsequent edition of this publication.

Contents

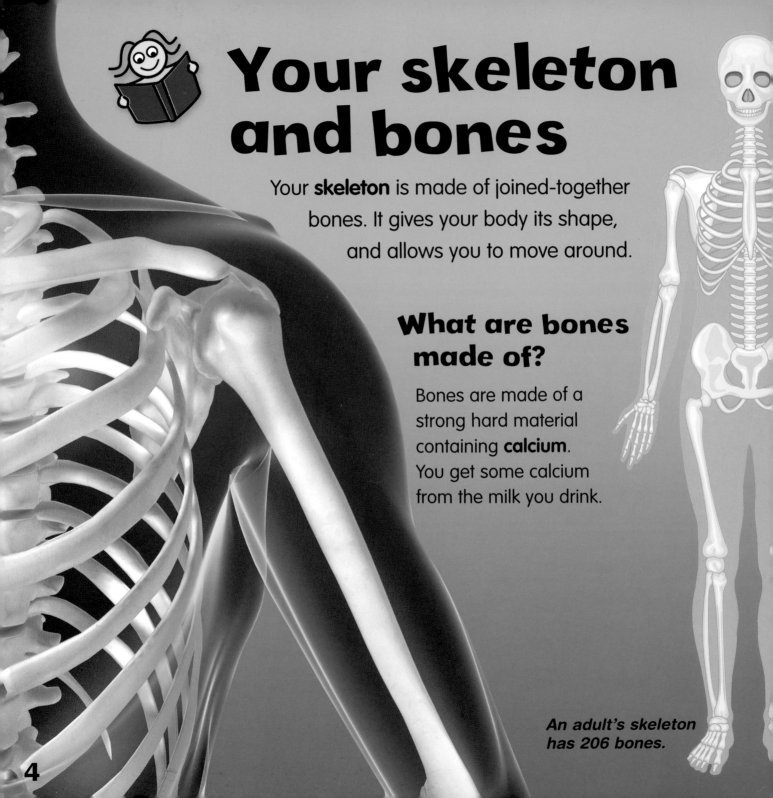

Your skeleton and bones

Your **skeleton** is made of joined-together bones. It gives your body its shape, and allows you to move around.

What are bones made of?

Bones are made of a strong hard material containing **calcium**. You get some calcium from the milk you drink.

An adult's skeleton has 206 bones.

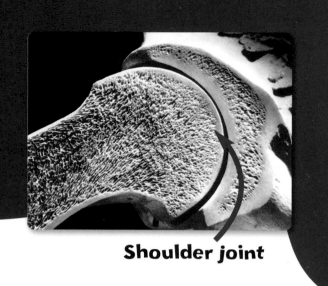

Shoulder joint

What are joints?

Joints are the places where bones meet. Your shoulder joint allows you to move your arm in any direction. Other joints, like your elbows and knees, allow movement in only one direction.

TaLKing PoinT

Which is the longest bone in your body?

Your thigh bone, or femur, is the longest bone. This long, strong bone helps support the weight of your body when you stand. The smallest bones in your body are inside your ear. They help you hear more clearly.

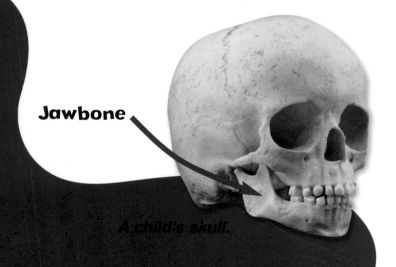

Jawbone

A child's skull.

What is the skull?

The bones in your head are joined together to make the skull. The jawbone moves, but other skull bones are fixed in place. The skull protects the brain and eyes.

Using your muscles

When you walk or lift something, you are using your muscles. You also need muscles to breathe and even to help you **digest** the food you eat.

Muscle strength

The more people use their muscles, the stronger and larger they become.

Some adults lift weights to help build up their muscles.

You have more than 600 muscles in your body.

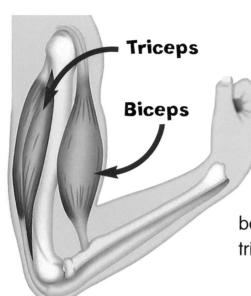

Triceps

Biceps

Muscles at work

Muscles can only pull, not push, and they often work in pairs. You use your biceps to bend your arm and your triceps to straighten it.

Muscle types

Some muscles, like those in your **heart**, work all the time, and you do not have to think about them. But you can decide whether or not to move other muscles, like your biceps and triceps.

Talking Point

How can you build up your muscles?

Eat a healthy diet and take plenty of exercise if you want strong muscles. Running and playing are good exercises for growing kids.

Sprinters have bigger leg muscles than long-distance runners because they use different muscle fibres.

 # Why do I breathe?

You breathe because you need a substance in the air called **oxygen**. Muscles under your **lungs** pull downwards, making the lungs get bigger, which sucks air into them. Then, when these muscles relax, the lungs get smaller and push the air out again.

You have two lungs

The lungs are connected to the back of your throat by a tube called the **trachea,** or windpipe.

What is oxygen for?

Oxygen is essential for life. Blood vessels inside your lungs take in oxygen from the air. It is then carried around your body by your blood.

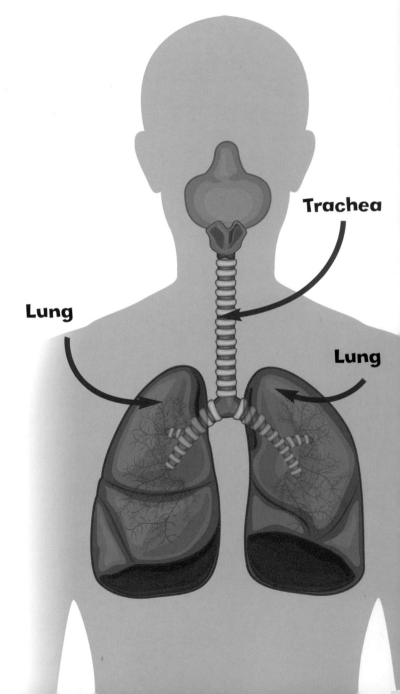

Trachea

Lung

Lung

Why do I breathe faster when I run?

Your muscles need fuel, just like a car's engine. When you run, your muscles work hard and "burn up" more fuel. To do this, they need extra oxygen, so you breathe faster than usual to get it.

It takes a short while for this runner to catch her breath after a race.

Is the air I breathe out the same as the air I breathe in?

Not quite. It has less oxygen and more **carbon dioxide**.

Talking Point

How can you look after your lungs?

The best way to look after your lungs is to exercise regularly. It's also important not to breathe in cigarette smoke. Never smoke cigarettes yourself, and try to avoid other people while they are smoking.

For people, carbon dioxide is of no use, but plants need it to live. In turn, they make the oxygen we need.

9

What does my heart do?

Your heart beats. You can sometimes hear it doing this, perhaps at night when everything else is very quiet. It makes this noise all the time, because it is pumping blood around your body.

Every part of your body needs to be given oxygen and other substances constantly or you would die. Blood carries these substances round the body, and it is kept moving by the heart.

What are arteries and veins?

Arteries are the tubes that carry blood from the heart to the rest of the body. **Veins** take the blood back to the heart again.

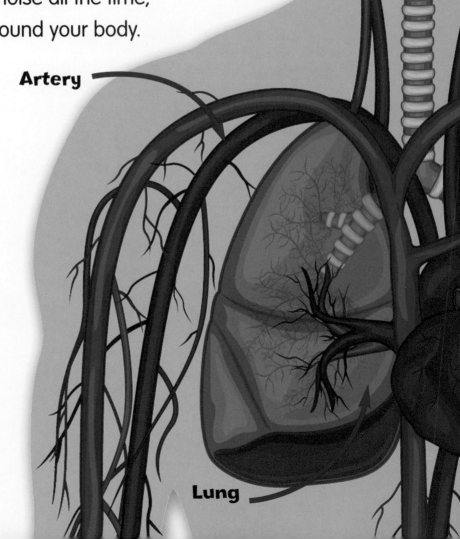

Vein

Artery

Lung

What is my pulse?

Your **pulse** is the feel of your heart's beat. With practice, you can feel it in your wrist or throat.

Use your fingertips to feel the pulse in your wrist.

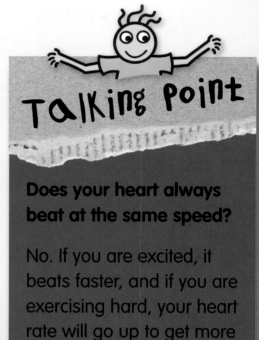

TALKING POINT

Does your heart always beat at the same speed?

No. If you are excited, it beats faster, and if you are exercising hard, your heart rate will go up to get more oxygen to your muscles.

WORD WIZARD!

constantly
All the time

What are capillaries?

Arteries are joined to tiny tubes called **capillaries**. Oxygen, and the other things the body needs, squeeze out through the walls of the capillaries, and carbon dioxide and waste materials squeeze in. The capillaries are joined to veins.

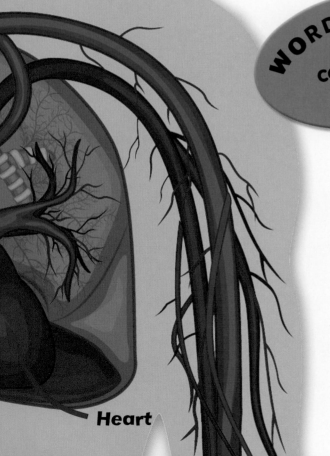

Heart

11

What am I made of?

You are made of **cells**. Cells are the tiny things that bones, muscles and every other bit of your body is made of. Even your blood is full of cells.

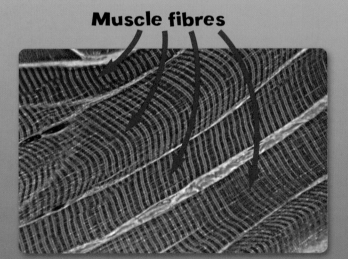

Muscle fibres

Muscles are made from millions of cells. Groups of cells form long, thin, flexible fibres that help the muscles to move.

Muscles

When you want to kick something, muscle fibres in some of your leg-muscles get shorter. This makes the muscles themselves get shorter, so your leg moves.

Bones

Bone cells are hard, making your bones rigid and strong.

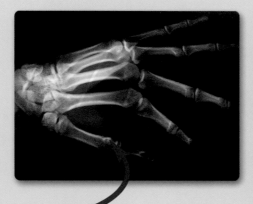

Bones

Bone cell

Blood

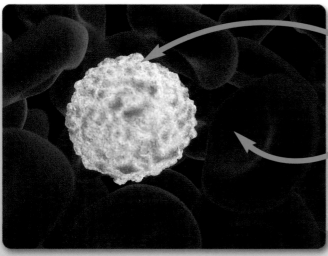

White blood cell

Red blood cell

Red blood cells carry oxygen. White blood cells attack the germs in blood that would otherwise make you ill.

Talking Point

Your skin cells are replaced every few weeks – what happens to the old ones?

They fall off! Every minute you lose between 30,000 and 40,000 cells from all over your skin. Don't worry though. They are tiny and you won't miss them. Your skin is also busy making new cells, to replace the ones that have fallen off.

WORD WIZARD!

rigid
Not bendy

Food and digestion

Starting in your mouth, food is mixed up with saliva and other liquids. As the food moves through your **stomach** and **intestines**, these liquids remove useful substances from it. The substances then pass into your blood.

Eat plenty of fibre to stay healthy – it helps your body digest food.

What happens in the stomach?

The stomach is a holder for food on its way to the intestines, and its muscles help to mix the food up. Water from food and drink moves out through the stomach walls into the blood.

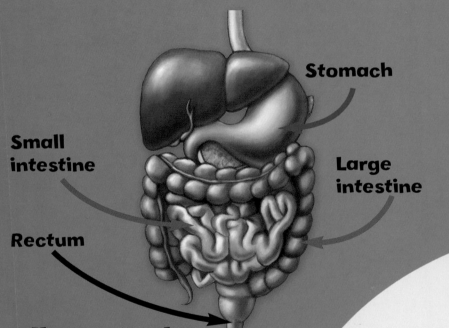

Stomach

Small intestine

Large intestine

Rectum

What are the intestines?

The small and large intestines form a single tube over seven metres long! It's here that most of the useful substances in food are removed and passed into the blood.

TaLKing PoiNt

What happens if people eat too much?

Eating too much can make you fat. Someone who is very overweight can suffer from health problems, so it's important to eat a healthy diet and exercise regularly.

What happens next?

When the useful substances have been removed, the waste ends up in the rectum. It is called faeces (poo). Your **kidneys** remove other waste from the blood. This is urine (wee). Faeces and urine pass out of the body when you go to the toilet.

What does my brain do?

The brain is your most important organ. It controls your body and works out what is going on in the world. It is where you think, dream, learn and remember.

How does memory work?

No one knows exactly, but people have different sorts of memory. Most things are remembered for only a few seconds – such as the words you are reading right now. But, if you see something several times, you may remember it for longer.

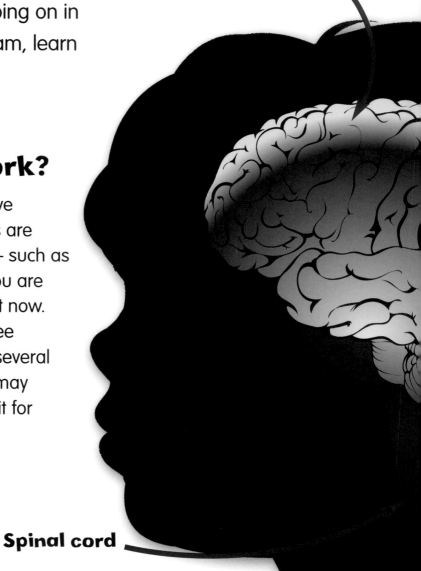

Brain

Spinal cord

How does my brain work?

The brain is connected to your muscles by **nerves**. When you want to move your toes, a message travels from the brain, down the spinal cord and along the nerves that go down your legs.

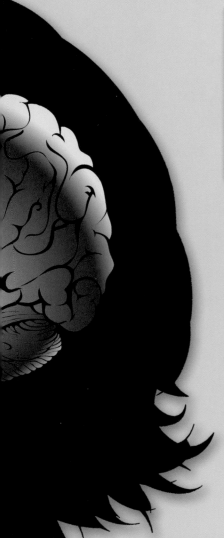

What are dreams for?

Again, no one knows for sure, but they may be a way of sorting out the things that have happened during the day. Dreams may help us to solve problems or get over things which have upset us.

Talking Point

Can you exercise your brain?

Yes, you can! Doing puzzles, playing music, making art, and reading books are all ways of exercising your brain. Anything that makes you think will make your brain work better.

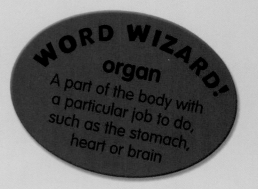

WORD WIZARD!
organ
A part of the body with a particular job to do, such as the stomach, heart or brain

How do I see, hear and feel?

Seeing, hearing and feeling are called **senses**, and they are ways of finding out about the world. Nerves connect your brain to your eyes, ears and skin. They send information about the world to your brain.

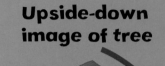

Upside-down image of tree

Optic nerve

Lens

Light ray from tree

Pupil

Retina

How does the eye work?

Light from an object passes through the **pupil** in your eye, and goes through the lens. The lens makes a sharp upside-down image on the **retina**. The retina sends messages along the optic nerve to the brain. The brain turns the image the right way up again.

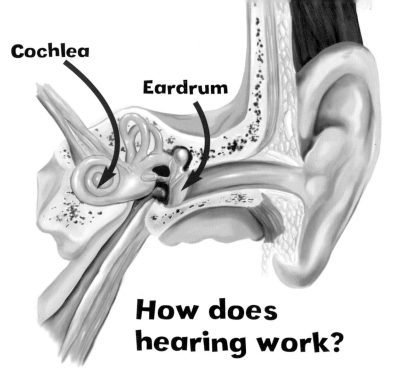

Cochlea

Eardrum

How does hearing work?

Sounds travel to the eardrum and make it wobble. These wobbles travel on to the cochlea, where tiny hairs pick up the wobbles and send messages to the brain.

Talking Point

What are your eyelashes and eyebrows for?

Your eyebrows and eyelashes help to protect your eyes. They trap dust and drops of sweat that might otherwise fall into your eyes and damage them.

How does the sense of touch work?

You have lots of tiny **receptors** in your skin that can sense things. Some of these receptors sense warmth, others sense pain and so on. Each has a tiny nerve connected to it.

19

Taste and smell

Taste and smell are senses, and they work in a similar way. If your nose is blocked and you can't smell, you may find you can't taste properly either.

How does the sense of smell work?

When you smell something, like a flower, many tiny things called molecules float from the flower into your nose and move onto a damp area inside it. The damp area contains nerves which send messages about the smell to the brain.

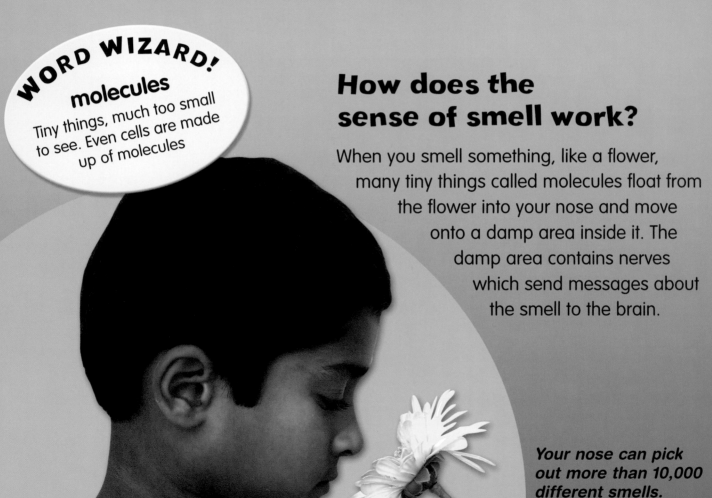

Your nose can pick out more than 10,000 different smells.

20

How do I taste things?

Your tongue has small receptors on it called taste buds. There are several sorts of taste bud, each of which tells the brain about a particular sort of taste.

Tongue showing taste buds

Talking Point

Why don't you swallow your tongue?

Your tongue is very strong and helps push the food in your mouth to the back of your throat so that you can swallow it. You can't swallow your tongue because it is firmly attached to the bottom of your mouth.

Why do we taste and smell things?

If something tastes or smells good, that probably means it is safe to eat. When things smell or taste bad, they are often bad for you. So these senses are very useful for stopping us eating dangerous things.

Food smells can make you feel hungry.

Do people change as they grow up?

As people grow up, both their bodies and their minds change in many ways. These changes happen more quickly when you are young than later on in life.

How does the body change?

People get bigger as they change from babies to children, and from children to adults. Their bodies change shape. People also get stronger as they grow up.

How does the mind change?

The mind learns all sorts of things, including how to walk and talk. Later, people learn to read, and later still they can learn many complicated things like how to ride a bike, do sums or paint pictures.

Child

Baby

Toddler

How long will it take to grow up?

Your body will be fully grown by the time you are about 25 years old. Your mind will never stop learning new things, but this will happen more slowly the older you get.

These teenage girls are not yet fully grown up.

Teenager

Adult

Talking point

Why do boys' voices break?

As boys grow up, their voices become deeper and stronger. This is because the voice box, or larynx, also grows. The larynx makes the throats of adult men stick out a bit. It is called the Adam's apple.

WORD WIZARD!
adult
A grown-up person

23

Glossary

Artery: a tube that carries blood from the heart

Calcium: a substance found in bone

Capillary: a tiny tube through which blood flows

Carbon dioxide: a gas that is present in the air

Cell: a building block of the body

Digest: to break down food in the body

Heart: the organ that pumps blood around the body

Intestines: the organs where most digestion happens

Joint: a place where bones touch. Joints allow us to move freely

Kidneys: organs that clean the blood

Lungs: the organs that we use to breathe

Nerve: a fibre that carries messages between the brain and rest of the body

Oxygen: a gas we take in when we breathe

Pulse: a small movement that can be felt in some arteries

Pupil: the round window in the eye

Receptor: a tiny part of the body. Your receptors sense warmth, pain, smells and other things

Retina: the layer at the back of the eye that reacts to light

Senses: sight, hearing, touch, smell and taste

Skeleton: the body's framework, made of bones

Stomach: the place in the body where food is stored

Trachea: the tube that connects the lungs to the throat

Vein: a tube that carries blood to the heart

Index